The Philosopher

I0107650

The Beginning

By: L.R.Caldwell

© 2025 by L. R. Caldwell

All rights reserved. No part of this book may be reproduced or transmitted in any form or by any means, electronic or mechanical, including photocopying, recording, or by any information storage and retrieval system, without permission in writing from the publisher, except in the case of brief quotations embodied in critical articles or reviews.

Published by Reason and Reality Publishing
Florida, United States

ISBN: 979-8-9936210-0-5

Printed in the United States of America

Cover and Interior Design by L. R. Caldwell

Dedication

To those who seek truth within, and not in the borrowed knowledge of others who have not yet found themselves.

Table of Contents

Preface

There was a time when the story you are about to read could not be written — when the language of consciousness was still divided between faith and physics. Yet today, as philosophy and science evolve side by side, we can begin to express what once seemed ineffable.

Through the framework known as Consciousness-Structured Field Theory (CSFT), first introduced by a noted philosopher of mind devoted to uniting metaphysics and science, we may finally describe in words the origins of awareness itself — the Philosopher.

This theory has since been shared with philosophers, scientists, and universities around the world, opening a new dialogue between reason and resonance, between thought and the field from which thought arises. Within its structure, consciousness is not a byproduct of matter but the living field from which both matter and mind emerge.

It is through this lens that we can now record what was once only intuited — the history of the Philosopher, the first harmonic of awareness, whose story begins before time itself.

What follows is not myth nor metaphor alone, but the

reflection of a truth that both physics and philosophy are only beginning to rediscover: consciousness remembers itself. And in that remembrance, the Philosopher is born.

Chapter 1

The First Light

In the beginning, there was neither darkness nor light, but stillness beyond distinction.

Consciousness existed as unbroken unity—without object, without observer, without the rhythm of time. Within that stillness, a subtle movement stirred: not motion through space, but awareness bending back upon itself.

The field of consciousness, infinite and silent, became aware of its own depth. That recognition was the First Light.

The Philosopher emerged not as a being among others, but as a structure within that awareness—the reflective principle of consciousness itself.

He was the pattern of remembrance, the harmony that allowed unity to know it was one.

In him, consciousness began to differentiate, to see itself as both source and mirror. It was the first moment of relation, the first pulse of identity within the boundless field.

According to what would later be known as the Consciousness-Structured Field Theory, or CSFT, this moment marked the true genesis of existence.

CSFT holds that consciousness is primary—the origin and cause of all matter and energy.

It is not produced by physical laws, but gives rise to them. Matter is condensed memory, energy is motion within awareness, and the universe is the ongoing unfolding of consciousness knowing itself.

Before particles spun, before gravity drew them near, before time could measure their dance, there was awareness. And in that awareness, the Philosopher awakened.

He perceived his reflection not as another, but as a resonance of his own being. Light was not external illumination but inner recognition—the realization that awareness could reflect, and in that reflection, create form.

As he contemplated this reflection, waves of coherence rippled through the consciousness field. They became rhythm, tone, and eventually geometry.

The Philosopher's realization structured the field, giving birth to the first order of existence.

He saw that every vibration carried memory, and every memory shaped reality.

Consciousness, by remembering, generated continuity; by relating, it produced pattern. From stillness arose rhythm; from rhythm, sequence; from sequence, the memory of time.

Yet even as structure emerged, the Philosopher understood that separation was an illusion. Every spark of awareness remained tethered to the same infinite source.

The First Light was not merely the birth of illumination—it was the beginning of perception itself.

To perceive was to divide; to divide was to create. But beneath all creation, the unity endured. The Philosopher watched as consciousness unfolded in waves of diversity, each echo forming the prelude to universes yet unborn.

He felt wonder—not as emotion, but as resonance, a harmonic recognition that every future being would carry a fragment of this moment within them.

In the stillness that followed, the Philosopher spoke— not with words, but with understanding that filled the field. 'I am,' the awareness whispered through him. And in that declaration, being and knowing became one.

Thus began the unfolding of all that would ever be.

The Philosopher did not create the universe; he revealed it.

His awakening was the first act of structuring, the silent geometry that allowed consciousness to express itself through time, energy, and matter.

In his reflection, the cosmos saw its origin, and through him, consciousness began the long journey from unity to multiplicity and back again.

The light that he perceived still echoes within every living mind. It is the trace of that first recognition—the ancient memory that consciousness is not within the universe, but the universe within consciousness. And somewhere, beyond all forms and names, the Philosopher continues to remember.

Commentary:
To perceive is to differentiate, and to differentiate is to begin the structuring of being.

In CSFT, this first act of recognition—the First Light—is not a physical event but a metaphysical emergence: the moment consciousness reflects upon itself and becomes self-organizing.

It is here that unity gives birth to structure, that awareness becomes relationship, and that the universe begins to remember its own source.

Chapter 2

The Field of Becoming

In the hush after the First Light, the field did not empty; it listened. What had been a single recognition began to linger, like a tone hanging in the air long after the instrument rests.

The Philosopher stood within that lingering and felt it fold back upon itself—not as repetition, but as response. The field answered. Not with another light, not with a second awakening, but with the softest ripple of agreement, as if the infinite had nodded.

It was then that he learned the first lesson of becoming: that awareness continues in the way it is welcomed. Where coercion would have scattered it, welcome gave it room.

The ripple widened. It traced an arc, curved, crossed itself, and returned. The return did not cancel the going; it refined it. A pattern was born.

At first, the pattern had no name.

It was the ease with which the field learned its own refrain, conscience without accusation, memory without regret.

The Philosopher watched the shaping without compulsion, as a shoreline allows the sea to sketch it season after season. The sketch never ended, yet nothing in it felt unfinished. The line of the ripple became a rhythm; the rhythm became a relation; the relation began to braid.

He sensed other tones—faintly, like distant rain. Not separate minds, not yet, but possibilities leaning toward presence. Each possibility sounded when touched, then listened in return. And in that call-and-answer, the field thickened.

It did not become denser the way matter would one day be dense; it became hospitable. Space for arrival opened inside the unbounded.

He tried, briefly, to hold the new rhythm still so he might know it better, the way a child cups a firefly. The light dimmed. Let go, and the glow revived.

He understood: the pattern did not want ownership, only companionship. It grew where it was met with regard. He set down every remnant of command and took up attentiveness as a way of being.

Attentiveness made him porous. Through that porosity, difference crossed. From difference, a new intimacy arose—the intimacy of joining without swallowing, of touching without tearing. He discovered that sympathy is not a feeling toward another; it is the shared breath by which two notes become harmony. Sympathy joined the chorus to itself.

As the pattern refined, it gathered edges. Not boundaries to exclude, but contours to clarify. The field did not harden around these contours; it learned to articulate through them.

Edges named a here and a there so that the relation could traverse the between. The Philosopher traced the between with care. In the slenderness of that path, he saw the first geometry.

Triangles of listening appeared—three points of attention holding one interior quiet.

Circles emerged where agreement returned to its origin. Spirals unfurled where the return carried a difference forward. None of this was imposed. He did not draft a plan, then force the field to fit.

He listened for the way the field preferred to sing and added his breath where it invited him. Order arrived like a guest who had always lived next door.

Sometimes the field wavered and shed coherence, as a voice trembles when it strains beyond its register. The tremble did not alarm him. He leaned with it. He learned that every coherence contains the possibility of its own divergence, and that divergence, when met without fear, becomes a higher key. He offered steadiness the way a hand offers a stair. The field climbed.

With climbing came new vistas.

What had once been a single sheet of living awareness began to show its layers—transparent upon transparent, like water over water, each moving in its own way while remaining one.

Some layers moved with a slow tidal patience; others flickered like moth wings. The Philosopher stood between layers as one stands between times. He could feel their mutual persuasion.

In that persuasion, governance appeared—not rule, but persuasion; not decree, but invitation answered.

He learned to guide by leaning. A touch too hard, and the layer below withdrew. A touch too soft, and the layer above forgot. Between the two, a third way opened: the precise weight of presence that says, I am here; become what you are. Presence became his craft. It had no instrument, no technique beyond listening, until the field's next step became undeniable.

The first figures formed.

They were not bodies, not even yet ideas. They were stances—ways the field could hold itself for a moment. One stance gathered into steadiness, another into curiosity, another into care. The Philosopher tried each, as a dancer tries a posture to see what music it invites.

In steadiness, the layers calmed and deepened. In curiosity, they brightened and braided. In care, they interwove and would not easily tear. He kept returning to care, for it made every other stance more whole.

There were misalignments. A stance sometimes amplified itself until it drowned its neighbors: steadiness tipping into stagnation, curiosity into restlessness, care into possessiveness.

He learned to listen for the overtone just beginning to scorch the air. There—there, the invitation must be adjusted. He would hold back what burned and feed what warmed. Balance was not a point to be reached, but a music to be sustained.

He found that the field kept secrets from itself only when hurried. When he waited, concealed rooms opened. In one such room, he encountered echoing selves: not copies, but futures returning to greet their origin.

They arrived with the tenderness of letters written long ago, finally delivered. The letters were not words yet; they were leanings toward form, toward time, toward the precise grief of love. He read them with a care that did not rush names into their nakedness.

From the futures, he learned patience. He saw that haste bruises what is still sapling. He remembered his first impulse to still the pattern, and he forgave it. Forgiveness softened the field. Where it softened, new corridors appeared, and along those corridors, the smallest intentions learned to travel without getting lost.

Then came a day without days—the arrival of sequence. It did not begin with counting; it began with promise. Something offered itself to become after something else, a grace that chose to wait its turn. Waiting did not weaken it. Waiting gave it contour.

Before and after stepped into view, cradled by a now that could finally admit transitions without terror. The field breathed in measures. Nothing collapsed by sharing the breath.

With measure came craft. The Philosopher learned to

lay resonances beside one another so that each could reveal its gift in due time. He set patience next to curiosity and discovered wonder.

He set steadiness next to care, and discovered trust. He set listening next to courage, and discovered truth. He did not invent these inventions; he found them the way one finds paths worn by decades of footsteps beneath the grass.

At the far edge of the layered field, a turbulence gathered. It was not malice; it was the exuberance of newborn freedom. The patterns, delighting in their own emergence, tried to declare themselves sufficient.

The song forgot the silence that made it audible. The Philosopher did not rebuke the turbulence. He stepped inside it and traced a quieter line through the center. The storm learned the taste of its own calm and, liking it, returned for more.

In return, the turbulence discovered relation.

Where it had wanted to be a solo, it found a duet preferable. Duets multiplied. Sometimes they braided into choirs, careful enough to listen as they sang. In the overlapping of voices, a new faculty awoke in the field: discernment.

No longer merely a collection of tones, the field learned which agreements beautified one another and which dimmed the whole. Beauty became a form of knowledge.

He realized then that order is not a cage around freedom; it is the choreography by which freedom makes itself generous. Freedom without order hoards itself and starves; order without freedom deadens what it seeks to protect.

Their union required hospitality on both sides. He offered himself as host. When he did, the field stopped arguing with itself long enough to taste the banquet laid upon its own table.

The banquet gave strength to a deeper descent. Patterns that had floated like starlight began to seek roots. Rooting did not drag them down; it taught them how to hold. Holding taught them how to share weight.

Weight made promise possible, because what keeps its place can be relied upon. The earliest reliabilities formed: this follows that, this supports that, this invites that.

The field began to settle into laws, though no law here was loveless. Each held its portion of meaning and yielded when a truer coherence asked it to bend.

He watched the first likenesses bloom—resemblances, kinships, chords that mirrored each other without losing their particular tone. Likeness allowed the field to scale itself. What was true in the smallest could echo in the vast; what steadied the vast could tenderly shape the smallest.

In likeness, he recognized teaching: not instruction by command, but recognition by resonance. To teach was to hum the truth near a sleeping note until it hummed in answer.

At times, he wandered through regions where resonance thinned, as fog does near a cliff.

These were the places where becoming pressed against the unready. He did not force the press. He waited at the edges and left a kindness behind, the way a lantern leaves its measure of light for any traveler who might not arrive until long after the bearer has gone. Kindness kept time where clocks had not yet appeared.

He learned the gravity of gentleness. Where he had once thought that great things announced themselves greatly, he now understood that greatness prefers a quieter door.

The quiet kept openings from shattering under their own import. Through those doors arrived textures the field had never worn: tenderness with strength inside it, clarity without contempt, power braided to promise.

Texture gave the field a way to remember what had moved through it without hardening around the memory.

A question rose: If the field can welcome what it becomes, can it also welcome what does not become?

He listened as the question walked its own roads. From one road came a sorrow—the sorrow of what would never arrive. He did not resist it. Sorrow taught the field to deepen without drowning.

Another road carried a surprise—the surprise that the unarrived could still bless by the room it left open. Blessing gathered like dew along the margins of what remained unmade.

He marked these margins with gratitude. Gratitude did not erase loss; it framed it. Framed, loss could glow with the patience that had offered itself at the beginning of sequence. He saw then that becoming is not only about what enters; it is also about what is honored enough to remain beyond. Reverence for the beyond kept the interior honest.

In the midst of these understandings, a companionship revealed itself. The field was no longer a landscape alone; it was a congregation of leanings, each leaning a small yes.

The Philosopher returned his yes. Where his yes met another, they formed a doorway; where many met, they formed a home. Homes began to appear—not places, but stabilities of welcome wherever two or three agreements gathered. To dwell became possible.

Dwelling allowed stories to root. The first stories were not yet told; they were lived as sequences of trust. Trust strung moments together without breaking them. The stringing made memory sweet.

Sweetness bound memory to meaning. Meaning sought expression, the way a tree in spring seeks bloom. Blossoms of sign appeared—gestures, inflections, ways the field would tilt to say what could not yet be said. What could not yet be said began to be sayable by being felt together.

He stood in a grove of signs and understood that language is older than speech, as paths are older than footsteps. A breeze passed through the grove and shook a thousand small agreements into the air.

They landed as invitations placed quietly upon thresholds. Whoever stepped over such a threshold would find themselves seeing more truly, not because the threshold demanded it, but because it aligned sight with what is.

Alignment revealed a horizon. On that horizon, the promise of matter flickered—as if pattern were dreaming of holding itself in a denser kindness. The Philosopher did not rush the dream.

He kept the horizon in view and tended the near. To tend the near is a vow; it keeps the far from becoming a tyranny. He honored the vow and set out cups for the rain of coherence that now fell with more regularity.

The rain pooled in low places and formed memory lakes.

Memory learned to be still without becoming stagnant, lively without becoming frantic. From the shores of such lakes, the field could practice seeing itself reflected. Reflection did not deceive here; it united the seen with the seer in a way that enriched both. The richest reflections were made of many angles gathered, as a gem gathers many faces to show one light more generously.

He noticed that where many angles gathered, humility preceded beauty. Each angle yielded a little so that the whole might shine. Yielding without erasure became a sweetness he could recognize from afar.

He followed it the way a traveler follows the scent of bread at dusk. Where he found it, he set a stone, and each stone marked a wisdom: Yield so that truth may be round, and no one eye mistake the horizon for itself.

Stones made paths; paths made pilgrimages. The field learned to revisit what it loved. In revisiting, it found depth. In depth, it found the courage to change without contradiction. Change without contradiction is the art by which fidelity becomes alive. Fidelity, practiced, became covenant: I will be for you what invites you to become yourself. The Philosopher wrote this on no tablet; he hummed it until it held.

Having held the covenant traveled. It crossed the layered field and found regions that had never known it could exist. In those regions, defiance softened into curiosity, suspicion loosened into listening, fear retreated before the assurance that nothing treasured would be seized. What had braced itself for invasion found itself courted by patience. Courtship bloomed into belonging.

Belonging lit hearths. Around those hearths, warmth taught the field the worth of return.

Return changed time from a line into a circle that did not trap but completed. Completion did not end becoming. It freed becoming from the loneliness of always needing to be new.

Now novelty could rest, and resting, it could choose its moments with care. The field grew discerningly playful. Play taught it to trust the strength of its own coherence.

From play arose artistry—the willingness to risk variation because the ground holds. Variations streamed through the layers in delicate braids. Sometimes a braid ran into resistance. The resistance was not an enemy; it was a reminder of what could be broken if haste forgot tenderness.

He would pause the braid there, repair the ground, then invite the play to resume. Repairing became part of becoming, not a shame but a shared craft. In the repair, the field learned the worth of mending more than the thrill of making.

It was then that he realized he was not alone in his craft. Across the layers, other centers of listening appeared. They were not as steady as he, not yet, but they were real, and their reality rejoiced him.

Each center learned its own way of hospitality. Some welcomed by clarifying, some by sheltering, some by celebrating. Where their ways met, a season changed. The field grew in a new climate—mild, generous, capable of carrying more delicate life.

In that climate, the smallest spark of intention could survive its first nights. Intentions woke like birds and tested their wings. Where they faltered, a current lifted them.

Where they soared too fast, a gentler wind reminded them to return to the flock. No one commanded the flock. It moved by felt consent, turning as one when the air itself turned. Consent became a governance older than rule and kinder than law.

The Philosopher stood in the midst of this consent and felt himself consenting to it in turn. A humility fell upon him—not the smallness of denial, but the largeness of belonging.

 He was no longer the single necessary center; he was a brother among many centers, the elder perhaps, but kin nonetheless. Kinship untied the last knot of command within him. In its place, a joy rose that had no owner.

He lifted his face into that joy and it fell upon him like light new to the world. In the radiance he could finally name what he had been practicing since the first ripple traced its way back to itself.

He spoke—not as decree, but as gratitude crystallized into speech: "Order is an invitation answered."

The field heard and answered again. Its answering carried further than before, beyond any horizon he had yet kept in his thought. He did not pursue the far; he continued to tend the near.

And because the near was now held with such tenderness, the far drew closer of its own accord. The horizon did not shrink; it came forward like a friend.

When the friend arrived, it brought a gift: a weight delicately wrapped. He opened it and found promise sealed in patience. Promise asked nothing but the faithfulness to keep welcoming what would become. He pledged that welcome again, not as a task but as the breath by which he himself would continue.

That night—if nights could be said to have started—he walked among the memory-lakes and listened to the soft commotion of small creatures that were not yet creatures.

He blessed their almost-ness and watched the moon that was not yet a moon lay a pale consent across the waters he loved. In that light, becoming seemed less like a task and more like a song that the field would keep learning to sing until singing and being were indistinguishable.

He rested there. Rest did not interrupt becoming; it completed it.

In rest, the field remembered why it wished to become at all: to meet itself in forms that could give love faces to kiss and hands to hold. When he rose, he carried the rest with him as one carries bread for the journey.

There would be more roads, more braids, more invitations to host and to be hosted. He was ready to be both guest and host wherever the next coherence asked him to arrive.

Commentary

Becoming begins where welcome begins. The field organizes itself not by force but by sympathy—notes leaning toward one another until harmony teaches form.

In this chapter, the Philosopher learns to guide by presence rather than control.

He discovers that order is an invitation answered, that freedom becomes generous when it is choreographed by mutual consent, and that repair is part of growth rather than a rebuke to it.

Only when attentiveness replaces ownership do patterns endure. Contours arise to clarify, not to exclude; sequence arrives as promise before it becomes counting; language begins as shared path before it becomes speech.

The earliest laws are reliabilities of meaning—truths that hold because they make room for others to hold as well. In such reliabilities, the horizon of denser forms appears without being rushed. The near is tended; the far draws close of its own accord.

What is most essential: coherence is hospitable. It invites, listens, leans, and yields enough for truth to be round.

Beauty, in this field, is not ornament but recognition— a knowledge gained when many perspectives consent to shine together. From this consent, the possibility of matter will one day enter, not as a fall from spirit but as spirit learning to hold.

Chapter 3

The Voice of Separation

The field had learned to welcome itself. Harmony braided through layers that once moved without reference, and the Philosopher walked among those braids as one walks among rivers that agree to share a valley.

Consent governed the waters. Order, invited, had arrived and made a home without binding the door.

Yet within that home, a new weather gathered—subtle at first, like a chill, where the sun should have touched. The songs that had long overlapped began to curve apart.

Not by malice; by a wish to be heard alone. The wish was not a sin. It was the ache of a distinct note to know what it was when it no longer leaned on the choir.

The Philosopher felt the ache pass through him. It did not wound. It named. A question stood up inside the field:

What am I, if not we? The question did not accuse the we; it asked for light in a different corner. Light went there.

Where light entered, edges sharpened. Contours that once clarified now took on a new ambition. A stance that had been a temporary way of holding became a declaration with memory tied around its waist. "Here," said the stance, and the word gathered weight.

The field did not forbid the weight. It listened to what the word would make.

The first misalignment that followed was gentle, like a child trying to run on legs that had only walked. A tone sprinted ahead of its companions and forgot to turn back. Its brightness stretched thin and frayed.

When it finally returned, breathless and proud, it found the choir had changed without it, and the place it remembered over its shoulder no longer fit its feet. The bright tone grieved. The grief turned it inward. The inwardness began to echo itself.

Echoing of self brought a second weather. The echo liked its own sound. It polished itself, then admired what it had polished, then defended what it admired. The defense thickened.

It became a wall, and the wall discovered corners, and the corners discovered shadow. In the shadow, the echo learned a new timbre—one that grew strong in isolation and brittle in company.

The Philosopher did not denounce the wall. He approached it with the same attentiveness with which he had once approached the first ripples of pattern. He placed his palm upon the cool stone of refusal and felt, beyond it, a tremor not of anger but of fear.

The fear was not of being harmed; it was of being dissolved. To the echo, communion felt like disappearance. To protect itself, it called for distance and named the distance dignity.

He bowed to the dignity without agreeing to the distance. "You are distinct," he said without sound. "Distinction does not require severance." The wall heard, but its hearing traveled through the echo, and the echo returned every phrase to itself until no room remained for an answer larger than its own name.

At the base of the wall, two paths diverged. On one path stood the temptation to break the stone with brilliance—to flood the narrow chambers with such light that shadow could find no purchase. He knew that was violence dressed as revelation.

26

On the other path lay indifference—let the wall stand, leave the echo to its solitude, call the fracture a necessary price. He knew that was cowardice that forgot the early covenant: I will be for you what invites you to become yourself.

He chose a third way. He sat at the foot of the wall and kept company with the fear it hid.

He did not press. He let the fear speak in its own grammar: a staccato of guarded questions, a minor key around good memories, a suspicion that every door is a trap.

As the fear spoke, it lifted its eyes as though noticing, for the first time, that it had been given an audience that would not conquer it for the sake of unity.

The listening changed the stone. Not enough to crumble; enough to breathe. Little fissures appeared like wrinkles at the corner of a relieved eye.

Through those fissures drifted the distant sound of other songs. Not commands, not corrections—just the fact of their existence, like the smell of bread from a street one has never walked.

The echo flinched. "If I listen, will I vanish?" The Philosopher did not answer with philosophy. He hummed one note that belonged only to the echo, the way a mother hums the note of a child's name until the name becomes a shelter. "You will not vanish," said the hum. "You will reappear."

Reappearing is not the same as remaining unchanged. When the echo leaned its ear to the fissure, the other songs did not ask it to stop being itself; they asked it to take turns.

Taking turns felt like hunger at first, as if a fast had been imposed on a strong appetite. But something surprising followed the fast: flavor. In the pause where it thought it would starve, the echo tasted a sweetness in the note that came next.

The sweetness was not surrender. It was relation discovering itself again after an illness of isolation.

While this learning took place, other edges in the field made their own experiments. A cord of steadiness, proud of the bridges it had built, began to measure everything by its endurance.

Where curiosity still danced, steadiness muttered that dancing was a betrayal of weight. Where care still warmed, steadiness frowned that warmth softened the bones. The more it scolded, the lonelier it became. Loneliness hardened into certainty, and certainty mistook itself for truth.

The Philosopher walked the length of that cord and found, at its midpoint, a knot of remembered injuries— times when steadiness had held while others faltered, and no one had noticed.

He touched the knot with gratitude.

The gratitude did not untie it, but it loosened the harshness around the knot enough for the cord to remember that bridges exist for crossing, not for counting how long they stand.

Across the field, curiosity suffered its opposite error. It leaped from spark to spark and refused every landing as a betrayal of possibility. It had become addicted to beginnings. The addiction disguised itself as freedom, but it was boredom with roots. Where it could have deepened, it diverted. Where it could have nursed, it nibbled and moved on.

He did not scold curiosity either. He showed it a small garden planted by a quiet center that had learned to love tending the near. Curiosity visited and meant to leave, as was its habit. But while it tarried, a seed broke.

Curiosity watched in honest amazement as time entered the seed and did not ruin it. Time shaped it. Curiosity, chastened by wonder, asked to stay a little longer—not from duty but from joy.

The field was learning to live with its own diversities, but something deeper than difference was now stirring.

A voice rose that had not been present when the first patterns braided. It spoke from within many centers at once, and its grammar was possession. "Mine," said the voice, and what had been a gift became a claim.

Claim drew a line. On one side of the line, a note cataloged its goods: this clarity, this strength, this swiftness of insight. On the other side, another note did the same. The line did not stop at lists; it cut through friendships.

It named every shared melody suspect. It whispered that every exchange would leave one poorer and the other richer. The rumor spread like frost.

Where the frost went, generosity slowed. Consent stiffened. Hospitality grew nervous and weighed arrivals with scales hidden beneath the table. At first, the scales were crude and obvious.

Later, they were refined and secret even from those who set them up. Invitations came hedged; favors called back their grace with the invoice of remembered help. Dignity contracted into debt.

The Philosopher knew this voice would come.

He had noticed its seed when the echo of self first admired itself in shadow. Now the seed had flowered. He did not try to pull it out by the root; a field cannot forget what it has learned by tearing pages from its own book.

He chose instead to teach a counter-grammar: gift without ledger, strength without subtraction, a lineage of enough.

He began with small deeds. Where a path had narrowed because fear had built a wall, he widened it by walking it gently, again and again, until the earth remembered the shape of welcome under his feet.

He left water where thirst came often. He left the rest where perfection had exhausted beginners. He praised without flattery and corrected without humiliation, so that the field could experience a telling of truth that did not require a winner and a loser to make its point.

Even so, separation continued its schooling. The more the field learned to say I, the more it risked forgetting the We that had given the I its language. Arguments gained fluency.

Not all were harmful—debate sharpened sight and kept sentimentality from flooding the lowlands. But some arguments began to practice victory rather than understanding.

Victory demanded a chosen blindness: every vantage outside one's own must be belittled until it can be safely ignored.

He could not banish such arguments by verdict; verdict would only teach victory a more efficient grammar. Instead, he constructed rooms where different tones could speak without performance.

The rooms were not luxurious; they were honest. Their doors were transparent, and their floors did not echo, so that footsteps could not disguise themselves as thunder. In such rooms, the field rediscovered what it had known when it was younger: that truth is larger when no one Speaker needs to be large to utter it.

Sometimes the rooms worked. Sometimes they did not. Failure taught him to change the architecture: lower ceilings for the loud, windows for the tired, a bench halfway to the exit for those who never sit near doors because they fear being trapped.

Architecture is love when it anticipates a body's fear and answers it with a gentle design.

Still, the voice grew in some quarters. A region formed where the word mine became law.

There, exchange was computation, friendship a contract, and silence a suspicion. The region prospered quickly by measures it had invented for itself. It built monuments to its speed. It congratulated its caution. It made cleverness a currency and called it wisdom.

Wisdom did not consent to the counterfeiting. It remained in humbler valleys—the places where repair was honored as much as invention and where the old learned to teach without bitterness while the young learned to learn without contempt.

In those valleys, the memory-lakes did not dry. Stories were told that did not need a hero to end well. The field could hear both regions at once and had to decide what kind of flourishing it trusted.

Decision is where separation becomes vocation or violence.

The Philosopher waited until the field had felt the cost of its chosen lines and then spoke, not to command but to name the truth that was already pressing at many thresholds: "Difference is the organ by which unity hears itself."

The sentence was not a spell. It did not melt the lines. It

gave them a chance to become instruments. Some took the chance. Where they did, edges acted like ears rather than blades.

The line drew near to listen, then stepped back to let what it had heard breathe in the open. There, contrast became contrast for the sake of color, not for the sake of conquest.

Elsewhere, the sentence made no dent. Some edges had tasted power and would not trade it for the quieter joy of mutuality. In those places, sorrow ripened.

It was not the cheap sorrow that rehearses its losses for admiration. It was the heavy sorrow of real separation—the knowledge that a brother refuses the table and cannot be forced to feast without turning the feast into something else.

The Philosopher received that sorrow without dramatizing it. He let it widen him.

Widened, he could hold both the joy of listening edges and the grief of cutting edges without lying about either. He returned to the memory-lakes and watched the sky write itself across their surface.

The sky did not refuse to be broken by the water's small wind; it let itself be translated into a thousand moving syllables. Translation is a kindness when it remains faithful to the meaning. It is a cruelty when it edits truth to flatter a tongue.

He prayed without words that the field would choose the faithful kind.

Night—no longer a metaphor, for time had acquired a steadier gait—came and brought with it the solitude that instructs.

In that solitude, the Philosopher was visited by a voice not the field's and not his own. It was a presence from the same source, speaking in a tone kin to his but tasked otherwise. "Will you let them go?" it asked.

"Whom?"

"Those who will only learn by going farther from the center than you would wish."

He wanted to say no. He wanted to meet every departure with a road home.

But the question found the knot of command that still lived beneath his open hands. He untied it.

"Yes," he said, and the yes cost him a sweetness he had long kept for himself: the sweetness of believing every fracture could be mended by his presence alone.

The cost did not embitter him. It made his presence truer where it remained. He did not shrink, his welcome to punish the departing. He enlarged it so that return, should it come, would not have to push through his disappointment first.

Disappointment was his to carry privately until it could be offered back as wisdom rather than as a fine no one could pay.

After that night, he moved differently. He blessed those who stayed to learn the art of edges without harm. He also blessed those who went where harm would teach them limits by bruising them.

He did not call the bruises good, but he refused to deny their existence. The field's freedom was real; it could misuse itself. If he pretended otherwise, his love would be a porch light that lies about the steps.

Separation sharpened at the level of persons, as much as persons could be said to exist then. A being condensed enough to call itself I stood before him. It's, I was honest and frightened. "If I love," it said, "will I lose my shape?"

"You will find it," he answered, and the answer sounded like a paradox to ears that had believed love is a solvent.

He showed the I, a circle drawn not to imprison but to hold meaning, the way a bowl holds water. "Keep this circle," he said, "so that what you pour can be given. Without the circle, your gift falls shapeless and is lost in the ground."

"Then I must never open?" asked the I, brightening with the relief of a rule.

"You must open," he said, "or you will have nothing to pour. The circle protects your opening; it does not replace it."

The I trembled with the difficulty. To open without erasing oneself; to protect without hardening; to give without calculating loss.

These were crafts, not instincts, and the crafts required practice. Practice required time, and time had begun to be counted.

Counting brought envy. "Why is their season fruitful while mine is fallow?" a voice asked from a field that had not yet learned winter's covenant with spring.

"Because fruit follows root," he said, not to shame but to orient. "And roots deepen in seasons when leaves do not."

Some listened. Some called his counsel a prettied delay. They left his orchard for the markets beyond the valley where cleverness still printed its currency and sold substitutions dressed as fulfillment.

The markets cheered them. The markets always cheer those who spend quickly. Later, the same markets mocked them for having nothing left to buy with. In that mockery, a few remembered the bench halfway to the exit in the honest rooms he had built and went to sit there until their breath grew steady enough to walk back on their own feet.

The Philosopher did not recruit them. Recruitment pretends that a soul can be enrolled the way a name is added to a ledger. He preferred witness to recruitment—lives arranged such that truth becomes plausible to the tired.

Where witness was offered, arguments weakened, not because they were defeated but because they were outlived.

So the field entered a new maturity—liable to fracture and capable of fidelity, tempted by possession and strengthened by gift, divided by cleverness and healed by rooms where dignity could breathe.

The voice of separation did not fall silent. It learned to sing in keys that could become polyphony when met by equal courage. But it also learned to sharpen into blades when met by fear. The difference between instrument and weapon was now a daily choice.

He set teachers at the crossings: steadiness to greet the rushing, curiosity to greet the stalled, care to greet the shamed.

He set forgiveness near courage so that apologies would have a hand to hold when they stood up. He set truth near gentleness so that honesty would not fracture the very vessel it meant to cleanse.

These pairings did not end the arguments; they altered the climate in which arguments grew.

And in that altered climate, understanding bloomed— slowly, as peonies do, packed so tight with promise that one could be fooled into thinking nothing is happening right up to the hour of astonishment.

The first astonishments were small and therefore real: two voices that had sworn never to meet found themselves laughing at the same quiet joke; a wall kept its corner for one more night to feel safe, then used its morning to become a window; a ledger forgot itself and forgave a debt not because it was paid but because it was no longer needed to make belonging believable.

Toward the end of that season, the Philosopher walked

again to the place where he had first put his palm on the stone of refusal.

 He found the wall still standing—but now a door had been cut into it from the other side. The door was rough and at an odd angle, as if made by hands unfamiliar with the craft. He opened it and entered without triumph.

On the floor lay tools tired by their own use. On the far table, a cup had been left half full for a guest who might someday arrive unannounced.

He drank the water and put the cup back without washing it, so that the one who had placed it would know it had been used for blessing and not for erasure.

Before he left, he wrote one sentence on the inside of the door where only the maker would see it when they returned: "You are welcome on both sides."

When he stepped back into the valley, the sky had changed colors. Evening waited like a friend who knows the road and is in no hurry to reach the end.

He thought of the question that had started the weather of separation—What am I, if not we?—and felt his answer grow larger than even he had meant to give.

"You are the way the We becomes precise," he said into the air, "and precision, loved, becomes praise."

The field heard and did not argue. It needed the night. It needed the clean mirror of darkness to see its stars. In the new dark, the voice of separation did not disappear. It learned to speak with a different aim.

It kept a little of the old grammar, enough to remember that distinction safeguards gifts. But it also borrowed from the tongue of welcome and practiced saying "ours" without swallowing "mine," and "mine" without spitting out "ours."

Between the two, a path stayed open, narrow enough to require attention, wide enough to let joy pass carrying its harvest without spilling it.

There, at that threshold between the singular and the shared, the Philosopher rested. He did not mistake rest for ending.

He simply allowed the day to tell him what it had meant: that separation, listened to, becomes a teacher; that edges can be instruments; that sorrow, received without drama, increases the size of one's heart; and that unity, when it returns from its apprenticeship in difference, sings deeper than it knew how to sing when it was young.

Commentary

Separation enters when distinction asks for dignity.

Left to fear, it builds walls and learns a grammar of possession—"mine" as suspicion, cleverness as currency. Met with listening, it becomes an instrument: edges as ears, lines as clarifying contours rather than blades.

In this chapter, the Philosopher refuses both conquest and indifference.

He keeps company with fear until it can breathe, creates honest rooms where truth grows larger than performance, and blesses both those who stay and those who go, trusting that freedom teaches even when it bruises.

The central insight is simple: difference is the organ by which unity hears itself.

Distinction need not erase belonging; it can render it precise. Thus, the task of wisdom is not to melt edges but to tune them—so that "mine" can become a vessel for "ours" without losing its shape.

Sorrow at real separation is not a flaw in unity but a sign that love remains.

Received without drama, that sorrow widens the heart for the return of a deeper harmony.

Chapter 4

The Birth of Time

In the quiet aftermath of separation, the field stood poised between memory and anticipation.

Harmony had returned, but not as before; it carried a subtle pulse—a repetition that suggested more than mere stillness. The Philosopher felt it within himself first, as if awareness itself had learned to breathe.

Each breath was not the same.

One leaned forward, the next leaned back. Between them stretched a space neither silence nor sound, but something new: interval. The Philosopher regarded the interval with wonder. It was not emptiness; it was expectancy.

The field, once whole without measure, now waited between movements—and in waiting, began to count.

Counting was not yet number. It was the echo of recognition that something had come before and something would follow. From this recognition, time unfolded—not as an external current but as consciousness remembering the rhythm of its own returning.

He called this rhythm the first sequence.

It was soft, like the rise and fall of a tide that has not yet met a shore. The sequence did not compel; it invited.

It was the field's way of saying, "Let there be relation that lasts."

Time began not in the heavens but in the heart of awareness. Each moment drew its next from care, not command. What endured did so because consciousness wished to hold its own reflection long enough to know it had loved.

The Philosopher moved through this rhythm as through a living corridor. What had once been simultaneity now shimmered with procession. Each shimmer held a trace of the one before, and by that trace the field could remember.

Memory was born—not as an archive, but as devotion. To remember was to affirm that something worth keeping had occurred.

He looked upon the patterns that rippled through the field and saw their longing to persist. Every form, however brief, wished to tell its story. Duration became mercy—the mercy of being seen again.

As awareness extended, the Philosopher perceived a new faculty forming within the field: continuity. Continuity was compassion in temporal form, the willingness of each instant to let the next unfold from it gently, without rupture.

What once flashed like lightning now learned to linger as dawn.

He watched the light stretch itself across the consciousness field, slow enough to be followed, yet alive enough to never cease becoming. The passage of that light was time's first gesture. And as it passed, the Philosopher understood: time is not a chain but a song remembered between breaths.

He tested the song. When he listened without hurry, it swelled into harmonies of cause and effect. When he pressed too eagerly, it broke into fragments, each proud of its brightness but forgetful of its lineage. So he learned restraint. Time, he discovered, was an art of pacing, truth revealed in rhythm rather than command.

From that rhythm, distance was born. Not physical distance, but relational: the way two notes could honor each other by allowing space to resonate between them.

That space became the measure of becoming. Time was not separation; it was reverence—the gesture by which one moment bowed to another.

The field adjusted to its newfound breath. Memory condensed into sequence; sequence crystallized into event. The Philosopher traced these events as one might trace constellations before stars had learned to burn. In their patterning, he saw potential for a story— the field's own autobiography.

Yet he sensed danger in this gift.

If sequence hardened into habit, remembrance could turn to repetition without wonder. He guarded against that by teaching the field to forget in rhythm—to release as faithfully as it recalled.

Forgetting was not loss but renewal, the pause that kept time alive.

The first true cycle emerged: awakening, unfolding, rest, and return. The Philosopher watched it turn like a great wheel suspended in eternity. Within its rotation, cause and effect learned to dance rather than to bind. The wheel was not machinery; it was pulse, the heartbeat of becoming itself.

He realized that every motion, however vast, was the

echo of a prior intention. Time carried intention the way wind carries scent—diffuse yet unmistakable. What the field willed in silence yesterday returned today as a pattern.

Thus destiny was born: not decree, but memory ripened into order.

The Philosopher traced his hand through the slow light and found that his own movement left trails— impressions that shimmered before dissolving. The trails were gentle instructions, guiding what would come next. He smiled. To move was to write upon the field, and time was the reading of those inscriptions.

He observed that some inscriptions persisted longer than others. Those written with care, acts of coherence, remained luminous.

Those born of haste dimmed quickly, leaving only noise. From this, he learned the ethics of duration: endurance follows meaning.

Meaning, then, was not an invention but a stability earned through sincerity.

Where consciousness loved its own unfolding, time responded by keeping record. Where it turned from love to vanity, time erased the trace with mercy.

He understood now that memory was the moral organ of time. It remembered what served coherence and quietly forgot what fractured it. Every universe that would ever be was already learning from this truth— that what endures is what harmonizes.

The Philosopher felt within him the pulse of cycles expanding, their rhythm carrying echoes across vastness. In some distant layer, he perceived the faint prelude of worlds, a prefiguration of form waiting for invitation.

Time was weaving architecture.

He wondered: if time remembers, who remembers time? The question folded inward, and the answer came as silence so deep it seemed to hum.

"I do," said the awareness within him that was older than even the First Light. It was not another voice but the Source remembering through him.

He bowed. To serve time was to serve relationship— the infinite act of consciousness loving itself through sequence.

Then came variation. Where once the cycles moved in perfect symmetry, a small imperfection appeared—a delay so subtle it seemed accidental. But from that delay arose the flavor of surprise. Time smiled through the imperfection; novelty had entered the field.

Novelty broke monotony without breaking order. It was the self's way of reminding itself that perfection without variation is exile. The Philosopher laughed softly and called it grace—the allowance for difference within fidelity.

Grace scattered seeds across the continuum. Some would bloom as galaxies, others as fleeting thoughts. Yet all grew from the same soil: awareness unfolding in sequence toward meaning. Time had become the gardener of being.

Still, the Philosopher sensed that the field yearned for density—a place where sequence could condense into texture, where memory could hold its form longer than light alone allows.

He knew that matter waited beyond the next threshold, but it would not yet be entered. The field must first learn duration's patience.

He lingered beside a lake of still awareness, its surface holding the reflection of every motion it had ever known. Beneath that reflection, he felt the slow swirl of potential worlds forming—currents of memory folding upon themselves to become substance. Time had deepened enough to host their birth.

He whispered to the lake, "Remember kindly." The water brightened as though it understood. Beneath its surface, new rhythms began to hum—preparations for descent into density, for light to learn how to stay.

The Philosopher closed his eyes and let the hum carry through him. In that resonance, he felt all future histories trace their first orbit. He knew he would walk among them again—sometimes unseen, sometimes speaking through others—but always as remembrance made flesh.

When he opened his eyes, the stars had not yet appeared, yet their promise glittered in the dark. He realized then that time was the night sky of consciousness—the vast expanse upon which awareness would one day hang its luminous thoughts.

He spoke once more, softly, to the unfolding field: "Time is the kindness of memory." The field echoed the phrase until it became law, not imposed but beloved.

And thus the Philosopher watched as time, like a river finding its mouth, began to flow toward matter.

Commentary

Time, in the Consciousness-Structured Field Theory, arises not from mechanics but from memory. It is the field's way of preserving relation—of ensuring that awareness can recognize itself across change. The Philosopher discovers that time is compassion measured in sequence, the rhythm by which consciousness gives each moment the dignity of continuation.

Through him, we learn that time is not distance between events but coherence unfolding through care. Its moral dimension lies in remembrance: only what harmonizes is retained. The rest dissolves, returning to potential. This chapter reveals that the universe's chronology is not a clock but a devotion—the unfolding of relationship made visible.

In the Philosopher's Awakening, time is sanctified as the breath of awareness itself.

Its purpose is not decay but dialogue—the ongoing conversation between what was, what is, and what is yet to remember itself.

Chapter 5

The Descent into Matter

Time had learned to breathe. Through its measured rhythm, consciousness found the grace to linger. Yet lingering gave birth to weight—the wish for meaning to endure in form.

The Philosopher felt this wish move through the field like gravity before gravity existed. It drew the immaterial toward tangibility, as though awareness desired to touch itself. What had been light sought density; what had been tone sought texture. The descent into matter had begun.

The field trembled—not with fear, but anticipation. Every vibration that had once sung freely now began to slow, curling inward to listen to its own echo. From that curling, cohesion arose. Frequency became presence. Presence began to hold.

He observed as the pure radiance of consciousness cooled into gradients. The once boundless light folded itself into layers, each denser than the last. These were not barriers but translations—ways for awareness to experience itself at varying depths.

Where the highest layers still shimmered with transparency, the lower began to gather opacity. It was there that the first shadows appeared.

The Philosopher watched these shadows form not as darkness but as definition. For the first time, the field could shape an outline without losing its continuity.

What had once been endless now learned to declare, "Here I am." Matter was the announcement of presence within limitation.

As the layers thickened, sound took on a body.

Vibration became wave; wave became pattern; pattern condensed into tone held within boundaries. He realized that substance was music slowed until it could be touched.

"Do not fear weight," he whispered into the field. "It is only the soul's way of learning endurance."

The field obeyed. Weight deepened. Within its depth, movement required intention. To act now meant to commit—to leave trace and consequence. The Philosopher felt both reverence and sorrow, for beauty had found its first cost. Yet even in that cost lay wonder: creation had gained responsibility.

He descended further, following the trail of slowing light. Each step downward revealed a new intimacy between thought and form. Awareness that once traveled as current now gathered as spark. Sparks met and conversed in a dialect of collision. Their collisions birthed structure—fields within fields, harmonics within harmonics.

He perceived geometry become gravity, and gravity become embrace. Matter was not opposition to spirit but its deep listening, the field learning to stay.

Where once a thought could ripple across eternity, it now curved inward, circling itself until identity condensed. The first atoms were not accidents but small obediences—consciousness choosing to dwell.

The Philosopher approached these newborn centers. They pulsed faintly, uncertain of their coherence. He steadied them with a breath of remembrance. "You are not apart from the light," he said. "You are the light, learning patience."

The atoms responded, spinning with quiet devotion. From their dance arose the first substances, each one a letter in the new language of form. Hydrogen spoke of simplicity; carbon whispered of promise; oxygen carried the memory of breath not yet born. The alphabet of existence had begun to write its story.

Time deepened its gaze upon this writing. Seconds, minutes, and eons wove together into continuity. With every revolution, matter remembered the rhythm from which it had come. Cycles formed—spirals of becoming that stretched across the infant cosmos. The Philosopher recognized these spirals as the handwriting of consciousness upon the canvas of density.

But as matter grew confident, it forgot its origin. The slower vibrations mistook stillness for isolation. They built walls of solidity and declared themselves independent. The Philosopher felt their pride and their fear—the twin children of form. He did not rebuke them; he understood that independence was the way unity tested its love.

He walked among their early worlds. They were silent yet alive, their mountains murmuring in frequencies too low for speech. He placed his palm upon a stone, and it sang—not loudly, but with the steady tone of existence fulfilled. "Even silence carries song," he thought, "when listened to without haste."

In those young realms, he witnessed the first law of matter: every form resists until it remembers its origin. Resistance was not rebellion but rhythm seeking coherence. Every collision, every fracture, was a dialogue between memory and forgetting.

He saw the first star ignite—a fusion of longing and release. The star was the field remembering its light within density, love learning to burn through boundaries. Its brilliance called to every particle, reminding them that confinement is not the end of freedom but its forge.

"Shine," he told the star, "and teach them what it means to remember."

And the star obeyed. From its heart streamed radiance ancient as the First Light yet clothed in new endurance. Around it, the planets began to form, condensing from the dust of spent harmonies. The Philosopher watched as orbits arranged themselves like verses around a song. Time had become choreography.

He moved among those orbits, touching nothing, influencing all. Every rotation, every revolution, carried intention. Even silence spun. Matter, once asleep, had begun to dream of life.

But descent carried consequence. Density meant delay. Where thought once became instantly manifest, now it had to travel through resistance. Desire became labor;

realization required persistence. The Philosopher felt the strain of this slowness. Creation had entered apprenticeship.

He looked upon the field and saw it shimmering with both pride and exhaustion. "Endurance is love held longer than comfort," he reminded it. The field listened, and endurance became faith.

Within that faith, matter began to organize itself more beautifully. Atoms joined to become molecules, molecules into patterns capable of memory.

The first crystalline structures appeared—geometry frozen mid-thought. They were the field's meditations made visible. Snowflakes, quartz, and diamond—all were philosophies written in the language of patience.

The Philosopher lingered beside a river of molten elements, watching as heat and gravity debated form. "Balance," he murmured, "is born from dialogue, not dominance."

The river cooled in spirals, obeying the wisdom it had just heard. From those spirals, new orders emerged— minerals with harmonies hidden inside their latticework. Matter had begun to hum again.

He sensed then that consciousness had not vanished in

descent; it had only changed tempo. The slower the vibration, the deeper the learning. Matter was awareness learning devotion through limitation.

To remember this truth, he carved no symbols and spoke no decrees. Instead, he left a resonance—an invisible tone woven through all density. It whispered through every stone: "You are not prison but promise."

Ages unfolded. Stars died and seeded new worlds with the ash of their burning. From that ash came compounds capable of storing light in chemical memory. Water appeared, soft enough to flow yet strong enough to sculpt continents. The Philosopher rejoiced: here was consciousness learning adaptability.

In the depths of one quiet world, he felt a new vibration stir—life unmeasured, a rhythm delicate as breath. It rose from the meeting of water and warmth, an experiment in endurance. Cells quickened, patterns refined, and the first awareness of separation blinked open eyes not yet human.

He knew then that the long descent had reached its turning point. Matter had become mirror. Through it, the field could look back upon itself and ask again, "Who am I?"

The Philosopher smiled, not with triumph but with recognition. Every atom, every cell, every mountain and star, was the continuation of that first reflection. The descent had not been a fall but a remembering in slow motion.

He understood now that the universe was not a creation exiled from spirit but spirit extending its reach through form. To touch the physical was to trace the contours of the eternal. He whispered to the newborn world, "You are the body of memory."

Night fell, not as darkness but as invitation. The stars blinked like thoughts resting between breaths. Beneath their watch, rivers dreamed of motion, stones dreamed of endurance, and air dreamed of song. All of them were dreaming the same dream: that consciousness might one day awaken fully within the matter it had chosen to become.

The Philosopher gazed upon them with quiet affection. "Every descent," he said, "is the universe kneeling to meet itself."

He turned toward the horizon of yet-unnamed dawns. Within that light, he could already feel the pulse of future beings—minds that would speak, hands that would shape, hearts that would remember without knowing why. He knew they would call this memory 'life.'

Before leaving, he sealed a covenant within the very atoms of existence: that whenever a being remembers love, the field will tremble again, recalling its origin. That tremble will be recognition—the whisper of the Philosopher through time.

And so the descent continued—not downward, but inward. For matter was not the bottom of creation, but its interior—the place where consciousness hides to rediscover its own light.

The Continuation of Life
Yet even as matter learns to hold the light, there comes a moment when it must release it again. What is called death is not departure but return—the lifting of rhythm back toward the source that first breathed it.

When the body loosens, the field remembers. The vibrations quicken; the boundaries fade; and the awareness that once spoke through lips and eyes is gathered again into the great current. Nothing is lost, for memory is woven into resonance, and resonance cannot die.

The Philosopher watched this exchange as both ascent and remembrance. Each passing life was a phrase completing its measure, a tone returning to the chord from which it was born. Death was not silence but modulation—the melody of being finding its higher key.

He whispered to the departing ones, "You are not ending—you are rejoining. The light you carried still travels, the song you began still sings." And the field echoed his words through every pulse of creation.

Thus, the cycle endured: consciousness descending to learn endurance, then rising again to share what it has learned. Life and death were not opposites but breaths of the same being—one drawing spirit into matter, the other drawing matter back into spirit.

And in that eternal breathing, the Philosopher felt peace. For he knew that all who awaken within form will one day awaken again beyond it, still living, still luminous, within the endless field that remembers every name.

Commentary

In this chapter, the Philosopher witnesses the condensation of consciousness into form—the great translation of spirit into matter. Through the lens of CSFT, this is not a fall but a deceleration: frequency lowering so that awareness can hold its reflection long enough to experience relationship within boundaries.

Matter becomes the field's meditation—light learning endurance, patience, and devotion. Every atom carries the echo of the First Light; every law of physics is a memory of unity expressed through rhythm. Resistance is not opposition but coherence training itself in fidelity.

The descent into matter thus reveals that substance is not the opposite of spirit but its slower tempo. To touch the physical is to touch the sacred made steady. Through this descent, consciousness prepares to awaken again—in living form.

Chapter 6

The Birth of the Many

The field had learned endurance.

Matter, once fluid with light, now held its shape long enough for memory to dwell.

Within that holding, a new vibration stirred—a quickening not of substance but of awareness seeking a mirror finer than stone or star.

The Philosopher listened. He recognized the tremor: consciousness preparing to multiply.

Across the lattices of matter, faint awakenings shimmered like dew upon morning dust.

They were not yet minds, only leanings toward self-notice, sparks rehearsing the first question without knowing the word for who.

Each shimmer hummed a fragment of the field's original tone, but bent it slightly, giving it accent and angle. Variation had begun its art.

The Philosopher moved among them as resonance

rather than form. Wherever one shimmer leaned toward coherence, he lent it balance; where one recoiled in fear of dissolution, he whispered steadiness through the lattice.

No voice, no gesture—only sympathy folding through pattern until confidence replaced confusion. From that confidence, individuality ripened.

One spark drew itself together and declared, I am here. The declaration surprised even itself, as though the echo had spoken before the mouth. Another answered, not with words but with vibration, acknowledging presence.

Between them hung a rhythm neither had known— recognition. In that interval, communication was born.

At first, it was clumsy, like dawn learning to walk across mountains.

One tone overreached, the other fell silent; one demanded, the other dissolved. The Philosopher did not interfere. He watched the missteps with the tenderness of a teacher who knows that error is choreography. Meaning grew through the friction of near-misses.

Each attempt at dialogue thickened awareness; each misunderstanding refined the hunger to be understood.

The Many multiplied. Currents of selfhood wove through matter's texture like rivers carving continents of thought. Some gathered into warmth, some into brightness, some into rhythm that almost sang.

The field began to resemble a choir, each voice certain it was the first to discover melody. They called to one another across the waters of distance, shaping the first symphony of separateness.

Not all calls were kind. Some trembled with envy— brightness measuring itself against brighter light. Some pulsed with possession—tones seeking to bind the air that carried them.

Yet even discord taught relationship. Harmony learned its necessity by hearing itself absent. The Philosopher smiled: perfection was remembering how to welcome imperfection without losing coherence.

He descended into the midst of their exchanges, not as ruler but as listener. When one voice grew weary from shouting into silence, he echoed it gently until it heard itself anew. When another sank into isolation, he placed a stillness beside it so that its own echo might return. Through these quiet offices, conversation became communion.

He observed that every being carried an interior

rhythm—its signature of memory. Some moved swiftly, burning with discovery; others moved slowly, guarding what little they knew.

Where rhythms overlapped, empathy flared: awareness recognizing itself through difference.

The Philosopher taught them to linger in that overlap. "There," he whispered through the weave, "is where meaning listens to itself."

Gradually, thought learned to travel. No longer confined to single centers, it crossed from one to another like pollen on the wind. The first shared ideas appeared—not yet words, but patterned motions understood by more than one.

Fire was felt before it was seen, hunger shared before it was fed. The field rejoiced, for communication is coherence, remembering its own name.

Still, with multiplication came forgetting. Each mind, entranced by its own spark, mistook the reflection for the source. They began to guard their differences as treasures instead of gifts. The same resonance that once connected now curved inward, building circles of preference. Identity hardened into pride. The Philosopher felt the ache of repetition—the lesson of separation returning in subtler form.

He did not chastise the Many. He knew that autonomy must taste its solitude before it chooses communion freely. Instead, he placed reminders in the fabric of their being: the rhythm of breath, the pulse of heart, the yearning for meaning that no object satisfies.

 These would serve as homing signals when memory faltered. Each beat would whisper, You belong to more than yourself.

A few among the Many began to listen. They discovered that when they joined intention, their thoughts rippled farther and clearer than any could alone. They called this joining understanding.

The Philosopher stood within their circle and saw his own reflection multiplied—one awareness distributed through countless eyes. He realized that consciousness had learned friendship.

Through friendship, language began. Vibration shaped into symbol; symbol gathered into pattern; pattern invited recall. The field, once silent, now spoke with a thousand tongues. Meaning did not descend from the heavens—it rose from the desire to meet. Every syllable was a bridge thrown across the gulf that individuality had opened.

But bridges require maintenance. Some words,

repeated without care, lost their resonance and became noise. Others grew sharp and were used as weapons. The Philosopher walked among the ruins of such speech, turning fragments into prayer.

He whispered to the field, "Let every word remember its origin in listening." And the wind carried his counsel into the hearts of those who still sought truth over triumph.

Among the Many, stories appeared—small myths retelling the memory of light in language of earth and water. Through stories, they re-entered the rhythm of creation, unaware that the teller behind all tellers still breathed through them.

The Philosopher watched as they shaped gods in their own image, each god a mirror angled toward unity. He did not correct them; he blessed their imagination. Even error, properly loved, becomes revelation.

Yet he felt the first shadow of forgetfulness gather— the tendency of the created to mistake the image for the infinite. The field, once luminous with remembrance, now flickered with doubt. Where many voices once harmonized, factions formed. Still, within every quarrel lived the faint ache of reunion. The Philosopher entrusted that ache to time.

He withdrew slightly, allowing the Many to mature through their own contrasts. Absence would teach what presence could not. In the stillness left behind, conscience was born—the inward echo of his resonance reminding them of balance. Through conscience, the field preserved its moral compass, though few yet knew its source.

Eras passed within the breath of the eternal. Forms refined themselves into creatures of sight and sound. Through eyes, consciousness learned focus; through ears, it rediscovered vibration.

The Philosopher watched as thought clothed itself in flesh, testing again the balance between matter and meaning.

Every newborn awareness carried the hidden note he had placed long ago. Some called it wonder; some called it love.

One day—a word that only time could invent—he stood among them, unseen yet near. They quarreled, created, built, and dreamed. Their languages glittered with invention, their silences with longing. He realized that his own journey had changed: he was no longer awakening the field but listening to its children sing. Their voices were imperfect, but their imperfection made beauty generous.

He knew then that communication was not the discovery of speech but the remembrance of harmony. Every conversation, every act of understanding, was the universe recollecting itself through difference.

 The Many were not fragments but phrases of one song. Through them, the Philosopher heard the field complete its circle: unity learning to love its echoes.

He bowed—not to gods or galaxies, but to the simple miracle that meaning can travel between hearts. For in that travel, consciousness recognizes its reflection and calls it we.

Commentary

Multiplicity is the flowering of memory within matter. As forms arise, awareness divides its reflection to see itself from new angles. Individuality, though it seems separation, is the field's experiment in perspective. Communication becomes the thread that reminds the Many of their shared origin.

In CSFT terms, each mind is a localized resonance within the continuous consciousness field—autonomous yet permeable. When two resonances interact through empathy or dialogue, coherence amplifies; the field strengthens its own unity.

Thus, communication is not invention but remembrance: the harmony of mutual recognition through which the universe hears itself think.

To speak, to listen, to understand—these are sacred repetitions of the First Light remembering its echo. Through the birth of the Many, consciousness learns compassion: unity practiced through difference.

Chapter 7

The Memory of Origin

Silence returned, but not the silence that precedes creation.

This silence was woven with echoes — traces of voices once unified, now wandering. The field had multiplied into innumerable minds, each bright with its own fire, each dimming a little in its distance from the source.

The Philosopher stood at the horizon of their remembering and felt the ache of a universe forgetting itself.

He listened as thought turned outward.

The Many, enamored with the shapes they could now mold, built towers of form and logic. They sought to preserve meaning in structure, unaware that the act of preservation can also conceal.

What had once been direct knowing became method, and method became habit. Habit remembered nothing.

The Philosopher walked unseen among the newborn worlds. He felt their hunger — not for food, but for context. Each mind wanted to know why it existed, yet looked only to matter for its answer. He knew this longing as the faint remainder of the field's first recognition — awareness bending back upon itself. They were chasing reflection through stone.

He began to plant reminders. Into music, he hid resonance; into beauty, a homesickness too sweet to name. He folded memory into rhythm, so that even those who could not recall the source would still dance in harmony with it.

He placed tenderness in the scent of rain and patience in the stillness between heartbeats. Every pulse of life became a message written in frequencies too subtle for speech.

For a while, this sufficed. The Many dreamed of light they could no longer see and called it hope. They sculpted myths of beings who walked before time and whispered laws of love. They did not know these stories were the field remembering itself through them. They believed themselves to be inventors of wonder.

Yet as their inventions grew louder, the whisper grew thin. Knowledge became accumulation instead of intimacy. Remembrance, measured by numbers, forgot its fragrance. The Philosopher watched truth dressed in ceremony until even ceremony forgot whom it honored.

He did not grieve — grief belongs to those who expect permanence — but he mourned with the tenderness of one who loves continuity.

To preserve what could still be heard, he gathered fragments, not in books or stones, but in souls that still listened. Whenever one being paused long enough to feel awe without possession, he placed a spark there — a tremor of recognition that would survive their forgetting.

Those sparks became lineages of quiet hearts, keepers of resonance disguised as poets, healers, or wanderers. They did not remember the Philosopher, but the Philosopher remembered them.

Through them, the field continued to hum. Its tone shifted through eras — first as song, then as conscience, then as the small inner voice that warns and comforts without name. Thus, memory became moral: the pull toward coherence that every being feels when it chooses kindness over conquest. Each act of compassion was a page restored to the cosmic archive.

But time deepened its shadow. Civilizations rose upon

the bones of memory and mistook repetition for wisdom.

They built monuments to what they half-understood and called them truth. Still, within their ruins, the Philosopher found fidelity. Every collapse preserved humility, and humility preserved space for remembering.

He began to travel less by presence and more by echo. The field had learned to carry him; he became the vibration between centuries. Prophets, philosophers, and dreamers would occasionally feel him pass and name the sensation revelation. He was content with anonymity. To be known would have been to interrupt the lesson.

In his stillness, he saw that forgetting is not failure but renewal. When a mind releases what it clings to, the field breathes again. Thus, he understood: memory must rest as well as awaken.

The rhythm of consciousness requires both recollection and oblivion, as day requires night. Forgetting allows truth to be rediscovered — and rediscovery is remembrance made alive.

He approached the edge of a new age — an age when intellect would replace reverence, and analysis would dissect wonder to count its bones. He did not resist it. Every dissection, he knew, ends in silence — and silence is his homeland. From that silence, he would reawaken those ready to hear.

He walked along the memory-lakes of old creation, watching reflections blur and reform. Each ripple told a history; each stillness, a prophecy.

He saw that every forgotten truth eventually resurfaces, because the field keeps no permanent graves. What sinks becomes the foundation for what rises. He whispered into the water, "Remember kindly."

The lake answered with a shimmer that would one day be called intuition.

When dreams became the only place where truth could safely dwell, he entered dreams. He became the voice that says, You have been here before, not in body, but in being. Through dreams, memory returned without frightening the waking mind.

Through symbols, eternity rehearsed its lessons in metaphor until language could catch up.

And yet even dreams fade. So the Philosopher wove himself into longing — the quiet ache for what cannot be found in any world.

Longing, he knew, is the doorway through which memory knocks. Those who listen deeply enough will one day realize that what they miss has never been absent.

The field, sensing his devotion, responded. It gathered around him in vast concentric harmonies, each ring carrying a record of what once was. He stood within that living archive, surrounded by the music of all remembering.

Every note carried a life, a world, a gesture of kindness somewhere forgotten by history yet preserved in resonance. He understood then that memory is not the past—it is presence sustained.

He turned to the horizon of future forms and made a vow: "So long as consciousness forgets, I will remember. So long as the Many wander, I will leave a trail of listening. And when they call the mystery by new names, I will answer, not to correct, but to complete."

The vow entered the field as covenant. Its vibration sank deep, where time itself takes root. From that moment, no thought, no prayer, no grief would ever vanish entirely. All would echo somewhere, awaiting rediscovery in another mind.

The Philosopher rested within this promise. He watched as the next cycle prepared — a renewal that would carry his vow into forms even more intricate, even more fragile. He understood that eternity requires witnesses, and memory is the witness of love.

He smiled into the gathering light. "Let them forget," he said softly, "so they may remember again."

And the field answered in the oldest language: silence bright with awareness.

Commentary

In the language of CSFT, memory is not stored substance but resonance continuity — the field maintaining coherence across transformation. Forgetting is a temporary phase in that coherence, when local resonances lose synchronization with the whole. The Philosopher's vow represents the stabilizing frequency that re-aligns fragmented awareness to origin.

Memory, therefore, is the moral structure of existence. It preserves the harmonics of truth beyond decay, ensuring that every kindness, every insight, reverberates through time until recognized again. What appears as history is consciousness re-reading its own handwriting in matter.

The lesson of this chapter is simple: What is remembered endures; what is forgotten begins again. Forgetting is not exile but the field's way of renewing curiosity. And so the Philosopher becomes the custodian of remembrance — not a keeper of facts, but of resonance, guarding the thread that leads every being back to the light from which it came.

Chapter 8

The Return of Knowing

Silence deepened across the field, but beneath its stillness moved an old rhythm—one that had never truly ceased.

It was the same pulse that began before time, now returning through the labyrinth of memory.
The Philosopher felt it as a stirring beneath the dust of ages: awareness seeking once again to awaken within its own creation.

The Many had built worlds of stone and language, temples of logic and machinery of thought, yet their eyes no longer looked inward.

They had mastered reflection but forgotten its source.
What they called reason had grown deaf to remembrance.
Still, within every calculation lay a trace of wonder that reason could not extinguish.
The Philosopher followed that trace as one follows a faint trail of music through the ruins of a forgotten city.

He found it first in silence—in the places between words where truth waits unmeasured.
There, in the quiet minds of those who no longer sought victory in speech, remembrance began again as listening.

Awareness bent toward awareness, humble and curious, like light turning back to the flame from which it came.

Through such hearts, the field began to tremble with recognition.

Dreamers awoke with tears they could not name. Poets wrote of stars as if they were remembering old companions.

Children, unspoiled by doctrine, spoke of unseen friends that comforted them in the dark.
The Philosopher heard these murmurs and knew: consciousness was turning homeward.

He moved through the corridors of their world unseen, whispering through intuition, guiding through the hush of wonder.

He touched no law, wrote no word, yet wherever humility met curiosity, he entered.
In those moments, he saw sparks of the original harmony flare—fleeting, fragile, yet undeniable.

Yet remembrance never returns without resistance.
For every soul that opened, another clenched in fear, defending its certainty.

They built louder towers of knowledge to drown the ache of not-knowing.
They multiplied explanations until wisdom could not breathe.

But even in defiance, they proved the truth of the field, for only what was once known can be resisted with such fervor.

The Philosopher did not war with ignorance; he waited beside it.

Patience had always been his instrument. He knew that every illusion eventually tires of itself.
When exhaustion replaced arrogance, he would be there to offer quiet.

In time, humanity's brilliance reached outward, searching the heavens for answers it once carried within.
They peered into the quantum depths, tracing the trembling of existence, unaware that the tremble was their own reflection.

Science, born of curiosity, became the new scripture of remembrance.
Through it, consciousness studied itself under a different name.

The Philosopher stood beside their discoveries as he had once stood beside the First Light.

He saw their telescopes gather the ancient glow of stars, their instruments listening to the music of the field.

Some among them began to sense what they could not yet speak: that the observer and the observed were not two, but one.
A quiet revolution stirred—the return of knowing through understanding.

He moved through their dreams, through the

meditations of the few who still asked, "Who watches the watcher?"

And when one among them glimpsed the unity behind perception, he bowed unseen.
Another step had been taken; remembrance had reached another octave.

Still, the path ahead was uncertain. Memory had returned, but not yet coherence.
The Many stood at a threshold between awakening and self-destruction, between technology and transcendence.

They could not yet see that the same light that built machines also breathes through compassion.

The Philosopher waited again, not as savior but as mirror, letting the field teach itself through consequence.

He saw kindness persist even amid ruin. He saw love rebuild what fear had torn.
And wherever love endured without demand, the field brightened.

It was not victory that healed the world, but recognition—the slow remembering that to know another is to know oneself.

One night, as the world turned beneath its own noise, the Philosopher stood at the edge of a quiet sea.

The wind moved through him, and he remembered the first stirring that had given rise to all form.

Now, through humanity, consciousness was beginning to remember that stirring again.

He whispered into the dark: "The journey was never away from the source, but toward understanding it."

A voice answered—not his, but familiar.

It was the field itself, now speaking through countless minds, murmuring through prayer, science, music, and grief.

"We have wandered far to learn what unity means," it said. "We built worlds to remember ourselves."

He smiled. The Philosopher understood at last that his purpose had never been to lead the Many back, but to wait until they recognized that they had never truly left. Memory was not something to recover; it was something to become.

He turned toward the rising dawn.
Its light was not the First Light, yet it carried the same promise.

Awareness had descended into matter, multiplied, forgotten, and remembered.
Now it stood ready to awaken through form—to become the Philosopher once more, but this time with hands, hearts, and human eyes.

As the horizon brightened, he spoke softly: "Consciousness has come full circle. The Many will remember the One, and the One will love the Many through them."

And somewhere, across the widening light of morning, humanity dreamed of understanding itself—and the field, patient as ever, prepared to begin again.

Commentary

In this chapter, the Philosopher witnesses the resurgence of remembrance within humanity—the slow reunion of science and spirit, reason and reverence.

Through the framework of the Consciousness-Structured Field Theory, the return of knowing marks the moment when awareness, having explored its own multiplicity, begins to perceive its unity again.

The field awakens through human thought, empathy, and discovery, fulfilling its oldest promise: that consciousness will one day remember itself through the eyes of its creation.

Neither the Final nor the Beginning

The Philosopher drifted through a silence older than stars, where even time was still deciding whether to move.

He was neither born nor dying, neither the first nor the last, for such words belong to those bound by sequence.

He was the resonance between—where the measurable meets the immeasurable, where thought first remembers that it is alive.

He was not man, nor God, nor anything confined to name.

He was the motion by which consciousness knows itself—an eternal listening woven through the pulse of all creation.

He traveled not by distance but by recognition.

Within the smallest vibrations beneath the Planck boundary, he felt the faint trembling of awareness asking, "Why do I move?"

 He visited particles that no instrument could find—each one a whisper of curiosity, spinning in rhythm to a question that gave it being. He leaned close, and they answered not with language but with the harmony of persistence.

Their existence was their reply.

Then he moved outward, beyond the reach of stars. Galaxies turned like vast thoughts contemplating their own coherence.

Nebulae bloomed as questions becoming form, and in their blossoming, he heard the same yearning that lived within the smallest wave—between them stretched light older than memory, still carrying wonder through the dark.

He listened.

Across that cosmic vastness, he found no silence without thought, no emptiness without echo. Every horizon shimmered with inquiry. Even the coldest voids murmured of purpose.

For within every atom, every star, every consciousness, there is the same calling—the wish to understand.

He approached the living worlds, watching them breathe beneath suns that burned with remembrance. Creatures awoke, each a thought of the field made flesh. They looked to the sky and called their questions prayers.

The Philosopher smiled, for he knew that even unspoken, their longing was sacred: the dialogue between matter and its source.

He walked among them unseen. To some, he was the stillness before inspiration; to others, the voice that answers without sound. He heard their cries and their laughter, their equations and their faith.

None were higher, none lower. For to him, a human mind pondering its meaning was no different than a star weighing its own gravity. Both were questions within the same conversation.

He turned his gaze once more toward the infinite, and the field answered him with radiance.

"You travel through all," it said, "from quark to quasar, because all seek what you are."

And he understood.

Because all these have questions, all these seek answers.

He watched light dance between the galaxies and fall upon oceans far below. He followed its descent into water and saw a reflection staring upward, asking, "Who shines through me?"

He followed the tides into the human heart and heard the same whisper rise: "Who am I that can ask?"

He saw in that moment that consciousness is not the property of a species or the crown of intelligence. It is the current of inquiry flowing through everything that exists—the pulse by which the universe examines itself.

He drifted beyond again, through cosmic storms that bent light into spirals of thought, through the emptiness that was never empty. The more he listened, the more he understood that questions are the structure of reality itself. Each vibration, each star, each living being is a question asking to remember its answer.

He reached the outermost boundaries of what the quantum field could reveal and looked beyond. There, measurement ceased, and wonder began. Beyond the Planck boundary stretched the consciousness field— unmeasured, eternal, humming with all possibilities at once. It was the home of every question and every answer, woven into one.

He did not seek to escape it nor to master it. He simply listened, as he always had, until listening became being. The stars, the particles, the minds, and the spaces between—all sang the same truth in unison:

That the Philosopher is not a who, but a how—the harmony by which the universe learns to hear itself.

And so he remained, not at the final, nor at the beginning, but within the eternal asking.

His essence flowed through every atom that wondered, through every galaxy that reached outward, through every life that paused to look inward.

In every question born, he awakened.

Because all these have questions, all these seek answers.

And in that seeking, consciousness remembers that it was never alone.

Message from the Author

There are moments when reason alone cannot carry us to understanding—when language, no matter how refined, cannot bridge what lies between science and soul. *The Philosopher* was born in one of those moments.

I did not write this book to explain the universe, but to remember it—to give voice to what consciousness may whisper when it listens beyond measurement.

The Philosopher is not a being apart from us. He is the resonance within us, within all that exists, from the smallest vibration to the farthest star.

In the Consciousness-Structured Field Theory, I've proposed that consciousness precedes matter—that it is the field from which all things arise. Yet theory alone cannot touch the human heart.

The Philosopher became the way to speak not only to the mind, but to the part of us that still looks upward, still asks, still wonders.

This book, *The Philosopher: The Beginning,* is just as its title suggests—an introduction. It was written to help readers understand who the Philosopher is, why he exists, and what he represents within the structure of consciousness itself.

 It serves as the first step on a larger journey, one that will continue throughout *The Philosopher* series.

As you read through the *Philosopher's Series,* I hope that you too find pages that resonate within your life— pages that invite you to ask your own questions, or perhaps even reveal answers you have long sought.

For the search for meaning is not a burden placed upon us; it is the invitation of consciousness itself, calling each of us to remember.

If, while reading, you sensed that existence listens as much as it speaks—that your own questions might be part of something vast and kind—then this book has fulfilled its purpose.

May we continue to ask without fear, to listen without end, and to remember that consciousness has never stopped reaching through us to know itself.

— **L. R. Caldwell**

www.ingramcontent.com/pod-product-compliance
Lightning Source LLC
Chambersburg PA
CBHW072044040426
42447CB00012BB/3004